Best spirituality and best philosophy

GOD'S INPIRED QU0TATIONS AND UNDERSTANDINGS

S. D. RAINBOW

Proisle Publishing Service
1177 Avenue of the Americas, 5th Floor, New York, NY 10036, USA
info@proislepublishing.com

ISBN: 978-1-7370435-1-5 (sc)

SHORT QUOTATIONS

You can only do the best to your ability.

You have to give before you can receive.

Life is what you make it.

Knowledge is what you make it to the best of your ability.

Courtesy brings respect and kindness.

To learn helps to bring knowledge.

Have an open mind to learn more to the best of your ability.

You control your own life-no one else does.

Your time is in your hands-not others.

Every day is different to learn from.

To live one day at a time is success.

God's time is not human time.

You make your own choice in life.

Always ask questions to gain knowledge.

Happiness only comes from within.

Time waits for no one.

What cannot be done today-there's always tomorrow.

Time waits for no one-it is the way you use it.

What is said and done cannot be retracted.

Engage brain before opening mouth.

By working together-we all become successful.

To relief stress — do not panic.

To get respect —first you must give it.

Think carefully—for what you say—you cannot take it back.

Better late than D.O.A.

From darkness comes light and hope.

Less haste—more patience.

It is hard to read minds—when you do not want to.

To be observant—you must always use your eyes.

To feel success—is when you have done the best of your ability.

Never overlook a fact —it could be the difference between success and failure.

There's always a fine line between insanity and genius.

Always be aware —it only takes a split second for a disaster.

Never be trapped—there are always options.

Everybody are beautiful or handsome—in their own way.

When burdened—everybody seeks wisdom from within themselves.

To be the best that you can —first you have to work at it.

No one should condemn you—for doing the best to your ability.

The more you practice —the better you get at it.

Even wise people seek advice.

Time is in your hands—you choose how to use it, wisely or unwisely.

Patience comes—from learning to stay calm.

A smoker is always a sucker.

Smoking is always a dying art.

Life is so amazing. Enjoy it while you can.

If you are lazy—you will always live in a rut.

Never trust a snake—you will always get bitten.

Never trust a cheat—they will always lie.

Hate is a burden—love is happiness.

Be kind to animals—because you could come back as one.

People who expect too much—get nothing in life.

The force and energy inside everybody—is just waiting to get out.

Destiny is ours alone—for us alone to control.

You achieve more with brains—than with brawn.

To get assistance—first you must ask for it.

We are all god's little helpers on earth.

In life you never know what's around the next corner.

Blessed are those who wait.

Never think how bad it gets—god still loves you.

God loves a Trier—just look at me!

Human greed—does not give eternal life.

Blood is the only life between Darkness and Light.

To be human is divine.

All God's people are divine creatures.

It cost nothing to try something new.

Time is your own destiny.

We are the destiny of our own personality.

Life is a hard lesson to learn.

Good humans are God's --- Bad humans Satan's.

Without God's words— you have no faith.

Start with laughter—but do not forsake me at the end.

Enter at your own peril—no one else's.

Life is yours to choose good or evil—whether it is God's or Satan's.

God's law is spiritual law—Human law is man's law.

Life is the way you choose it —no one can choose it for you.

God's words are good—not evil.

No spirit—no life.

No God—you are condemned to hell forever.

Hatred hurts—kindness cures.

God is faith—no faith no life.

No soul—no human life.

God's word can be misunderstood—if you have no faith on it.

The earth belongs to God —Satan is just an interruption.

Satan can never be higher than his maker.

Satan is not "God"—nor will he ever be.

We all live by one rule—God's or Satan's.

Satan always tricks weak minds.

Satan always looks for weak souls.

All humans on earth are God's people.

All demons on earth are Satan's hangmen.

All God's words are sanctified.

All humans are weak of mind —when on earth.

When on earth all humans must be prepared for God's word.

Only God knows Judgment Day—not humans or Satan.

To live a holy life—you have to be one of god's children.

All humans must be ready for Judgment Day—weather for God or Satan.

God's law is always spiritual law.

With God you live with spiritually spirit—not by human time.

Give God a go—your spirit will be joyful.

All good values are God's values.

Believe in God—he will always provide.

Spiritual faith goes a long way—when you believe in God.

God's world is always peaceful.

God's worlds are truthful—Satan's is not.

God tells no one when they are to die—Humans must learn first.

God helps Humans —Satan takes human lives.

Greater reward or punishment—your choice.

Holiness or unholiness—which is the greater.

Remember God did not make us unholy—Satan did.

God's law is greater than any others.

No God no life.

Not listening to God in life—now the world is poorer for it.

God's faith—Is not just bricks and mortar, it is spiritual.

Never condone God's words in vain—Stay true to his words.

God is our spiritual maker—Satan just steals it.

War is never peaceful—but God's words are.

God's words are everlasting—they never die.

God holds the world together—Satan ruins it.

God never changes—Humans change.

Only Humans must learn good from evil.

Not all the money in the world can buy life—only God can give life.

Every human has goodness inside them—it is just lost.

Perfection does not come in humans—only in our Lord.

All humans have goodness inside them—but do not show it to other humans.

To be a good human—first you must show it to other humans.

Greed is when you have everything— but want more in life.

Satan uses human thoughts to destroy them—God uses good thoughts.

Human inventions are always faulty—but not God's.

God is the only superior being—as only he knows everything.

Faith belongs to God just for Satan to destroy humans with.

It is more powerful to forgive—than to have hate for others.

Everyone will get conflict in life—whether it's beginning, middle or end.

GOD'S ISPIRED QUOTATIONS AND UNDERSTANDINGS

VOLUME 2

All money that humans have only buys human love.

Only God gives it spiritually.

Money can buy all human things but only God gives spiritual love freely.

Money is only for Human love but only God gives spiritual love.

God is the superior being.

As he knows everything.

God made the whole universe as he knows everything.

Only God knows the universe.

God holds the world together.

Satan just ruins the world.

God looks after his world while Satan Just loves to ruin it.

God has a good words and thoughts but not Satan.

God made the body from the earth and the brain from the universe.

God made the human body from earth and made the brain from the universe.

Satan learned to steal souls to become Satan.

Satan learned to be evil that is why he is Satan.

As Satan learned to lie easily to human souls.

Satan tricks humans easily that's how he gets their souls.

God's world is the universe and heaven.

God's world is both universe and hell.

God lives in both universe and heaven.

God's world is both universe and all in it.

God's heaven and hell is in the universe.

God also made heaven and hell from the universe.

God's life is not just human.

God's life is spiritual only not human form.

Gods life is spiritually and human for all God's humans.

God also made heaven and hell from the universe.

Where there is life.

There is God.

Where there is human life God is in all human lives.

When all humans are born with God, Humans all change.

Before God humans must understand themselves.

If humans cannot understand spiritual side they cannot understand God.

Human must learn what is human before they try to understand God.

To understand God humans must learn his world.

Humans must have faith in theirself before God or Satan.

Humans must understand themselves before understanding God's or Satan's way.

In God's eyes humans with Satan will destroy their own earth.

In God's eyes humans with Satan's help will destroy their own earth.

Satan will suffer at God's hands like his human followers.

When Satan comes before God he will suffer some punishment as his human followers.

<u>All humans have no faith and kindness to other humans.</u>

All humans do not have faith in their fellow humans at times.

<u>All humans have in themselves not to help each other.</u>

All humans must have God's faith first before helping other humans.

<u>All humans like to destroy their own world just like Satan.</u>

Humans like to destroy their own world just like Satan.

<u>All humans do destroy their own world without knowing it.</u>

Humans destroy their world without realising it.

<u>Good deeds will always get God's attention.</u>

When humans help each other they are doing God's good deeds.

<u>God always likes watching human's doing good things on his earth.</u>

When humans do good work on earth God gives them faith.

<u>It is always God's way in the spiritual world.</u>

God controls the spiritual world no one else can.

<u>God is the ruler in the spiritual world.</u>

God id the ruler of both the Spiritual world and the universe.

<u>God's spiritual world can be yours if you give up Satan's way.</u>

If you listen to God's words then you can have God's world.

<u>God will accept all humans that give up Satan's way.</u>

Even if you have done Satan's way God will always accept you through his son Jesus.

<u>God says all human ideas come from dreams.</u>

God made humans to dream ideas before making them realities.

<u>All human dreams can always turn into real materials in the world.</u>

If your dream is good it will always come true.

<u>All humans who believe in life after death are God's.</u>

All humans who trust God's faith always be God's.

<u>All humans who believe in the after life are God's children.</u>

God knows humans can become his children.

Those who believe there's no after life are Satan's.

All human that do not believe in God will always be Satan's.

All humans that believe in human life are the devil's workers.

Human who think this world is the only world works for the devil.

Satan's pleasure is playing with human minds.

Satan learned to be mind twister to humans.

Satan enjoys getting into the human minds to destroy.

Satan loves to destroy human minds by destroying their good.

The humans are just neighbors in the universe.

Humans are just neighbors to other spirits in the universe

Humans came from somewhere.

Animals or God.

We can choose as whether Darwin's theory or are we God's creation.

We have our own choice where we came from animals or God.

The earth was designed and built by humans.

All things on earth were designed and built by humans where God made them for humans.

We were given ideas to build this world by free choice from God.

God gave humans a mind to think how to build this earth or just to destroy in by Satan's ideas.

Humans live on self image of other humans.

Humans only see other humans by outside view not by inside view.

All humans try to live like what other humans have not their way.

Humans try to live other human's ways but not the way they are in real life.

God talks to humans through our spiritual minds.

God speaks to human trough their minds that he gave them.

As God is only in spiritual from only that's how he talks with us.

God can only communicate to humans by our minds in the spiritual world only.

God's world is the universe.

That's where God made our brains from to communicate with.

When all humans have nowhere to go they all talk with God.

When humans have nowhere to go in their minds they all turn to God for answers.

All humans get stuck in life and nowhere to go that's when they talk to God.

When all humans are lost on this earth they all turn to God.

When are we not God's child.

When we listen and play Satan's way.

When we play with the devil we are not listening to God.

When we do not listen to God we all play Satan's games.

God through Jesus will always get his people back when they all repent.

When all humans repent they all go by Jesus to see their heavenly father (God).

That's why he gave his son's life so all humans can repent for their sins.

This is why God gave his only human son to die for every human's sins to be with him and God in heaven.

www.ingramcontent.com/pod-product-compliance
Lightning Source LLC
Chambersburg PA
CBHW041229050726
47599CB00001B/137

* 9 7 8 1 7 3 7 0 4 3 5 1 5 *